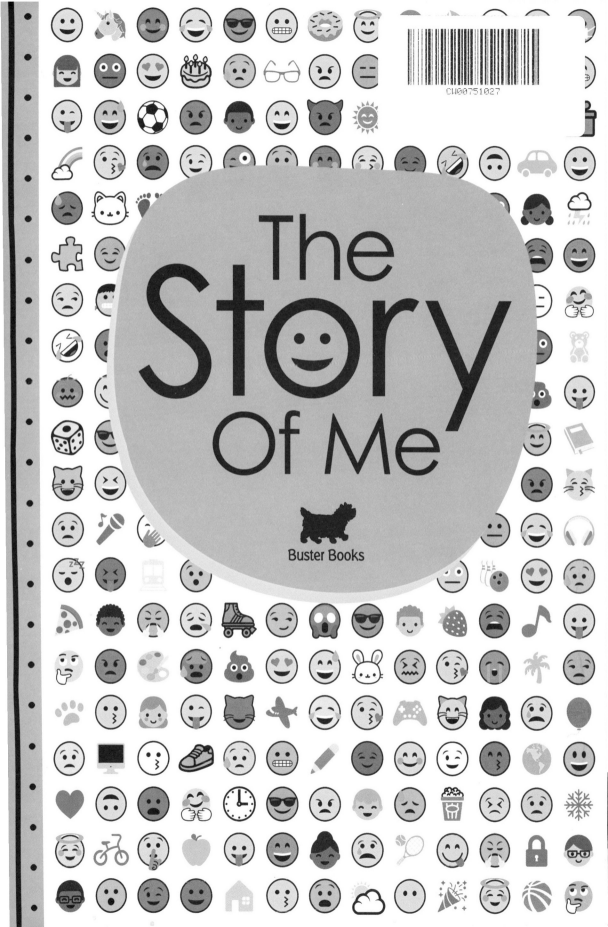

The Story Of Me

Buster Books

WRITTEN BY
ELLEN BAILEY

EDITED BY EMMA TAYLOR

DESIGNED BY DERRIAN BRADDER
AND JANENE SPENCER

COVER DESIGNED BY ANGIE ALLISON
AND ZOE BRADLEY

WITH CONTRIBUTIONS BY
ISLA MAY NOWAK, AGE 8

The Story Of Me

Buster Books

First published in Great Britain in 2022 by Buster Books, an imprint of
Michael O'Mara Books Limited, 9 Lion Yard, Tremadoc Road, London SW4 7NQ

 www.mombooks.com/buster   Buster Books   @BusterBooks   @buster_books

ISBN: 978-1-78055-795-3

1 3 5 7 9 10 8 6 4 2

This book was printed in December 2021 by Shenzhen Wing King
Tong Paper Products Co. Ltd., Shenzhen, Guangdong, China.

CONTENTS

THIS BOOK BELONGS TO:

....

....

INTRODUCTION

Welcome to your personal memory book. Inside, you'll find tons of quizzes and questions that will help you make a lasting record of who you are. From the day you were born to your dreams for the future — and everything in-between — there's plenty of space for you to write all about your life.

You don't have to complete this book in any particular order. Just find a page that fits your mood and the moment. There are pages to colour, draw, design and fill in as well as lots of awesome quotes to help motivate and inspire you.

So grab your pens and pencils and start filling in YOUR STORY!

CHAPTER 1:
THE BEGINNING

This first chapter is a space for you to record everything about how you came into the world and your first year of life. If there are questions that you can't find the answer to, don't worry — just fill in what you can.

If there's no one you can ask, perhaps you could imagine what life was like when you were a baby and use your imagination to fill in the gaps.

YOUR BIRTH FACT FILE

Use these pages to make a record
of the day you were born.

WHAT DATE WERE YOU BORN?

WHAT TIME OF THE DAY WAS IT?

WHAT IS YOUR STAR SIGN?

WHAT NAME WERE YOU GIVEN?
Remember to include your middle
name(s) if you have one.

WHERE WERE YOU BORN?
Write the name of the hospital or
the location of where you were born.

HOW MUCH DID YOU WEIGH?

POUNDS   OUNCES

WHAT WAS THE WEATHER LIKE?
Was it blue skies and sunshine
or was it cloudy and raining?

WHAT SONG WAS NO. 1 ON THE DAY YOU WERE BORN?

WHAT DID YOU LOOK LIKE?
How much hair did you have?
What colour was it?

WHO ELSE WAS THERE ON
THE DAY YOU WERE BORN?

PICTURE PERFECT

Hunt for the earliest photo of yourself that you can find and stick a copy in the frame below. If you can't find a photo, draw a picture of yourself as a newborn baby. Write a caption to describe the picture in the space below the frame.

BABY FIRSTS

FIRST TOYS
What were they? Who gave them to you? Do you still have them?

FIRST FOOD
What was it? Did you like it?

FIRST STEPS
Where were you? Who was there? How old were you?

FIRST WORDS
What did you say? How old were you?

FIRST SHOES
What were they like? Which shop did they come from?

FIRST TOOTH
How old were you? Did the feeling of it coming through make you grumpy?

FIRST HAIRCUT
How old were you?

BABY STORIES

Do you know any funny stories from when you were a baby? Keep a record of them on the pages of these books. You can do this either in writing or by drawing pictures. If you don't already know any stories, perhaps you could speak to some people who knew you when you were a baby and ask them about their memories of you.

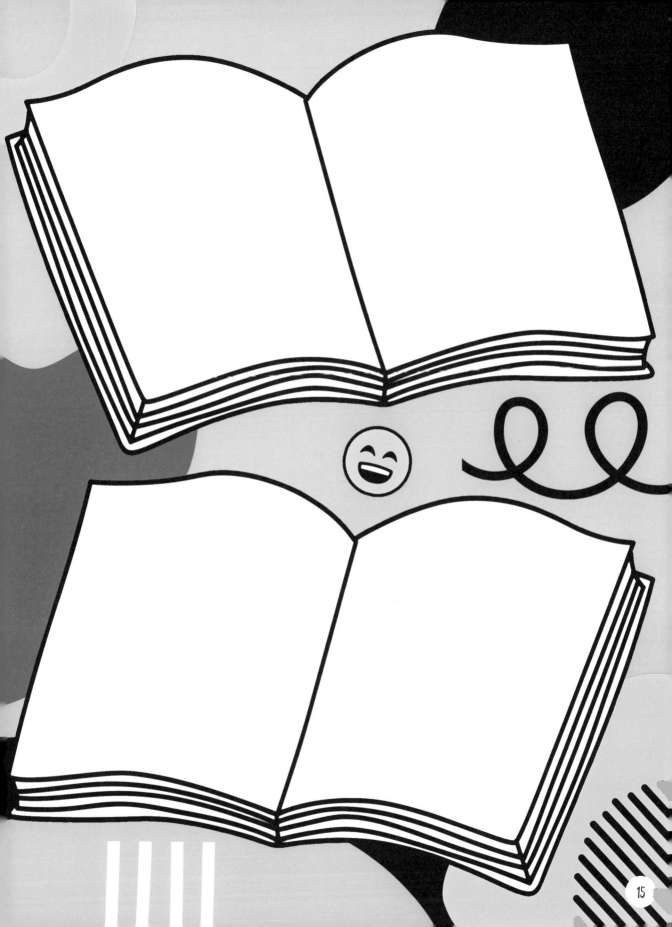

BABY NAMES

Did your parents have ideas for other names they might have called you? Write a list of them below. If you're not sure, add some other names that you would have liked to have been called.

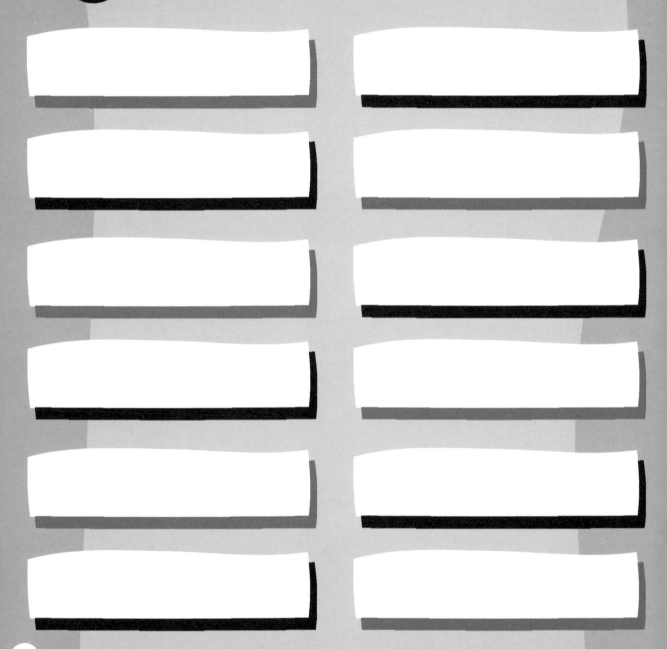

BABY LOVE

Babies can have strong opinions about what they like and don't like. Use a pen to colour in the hearts of the things you loved when you were a baby. If there's anything here you really didn't like, cross the heart out.

LULLABIES

TRAVELLING BY CAR

DUMMIES

BEING TICKLED

BATH TIME

ANIMALS

PLAYING PEEKABOO

LOUD NOISES

BANANAS

SEEING YOUR REFLECTION IN A MIRROR

GOING TO THE DOCTOR

HAVING YOUR NAPPY CHANGED

BABY BUDDIES

Fill these frames with photos or drawings of the other babies you played with when you were little. Write the name of each friend in the space below and colour in the rattle if you're still friends with them now.

BABY CLOTHES

What clothes did you wear when you were a baby? Did your parents have a favourite outfit for you? Draw a picture of it in the space below and write down why it was their favourite. If they didn't have a favourite, why not try designing your own outfit?

GOO GOO GAMES

What were your favourite games when you were a baby? Perhaps you loved playing with bath toys or being swung around like an aeroplane. Draw or write in the spaces below to create a record of the games you used to love. Can you remember any nursery rhymes or songs you used to sing? Write down the words so you never forget them.

NURSERY RHYME:

NURSERY RHYME:

NURSERY RHYME:

EARLIEST MEMORY

What is the very first thing you can remember happening in your life? Draw a picture of it in the space below then write a few lines to describe what happened.

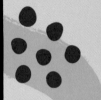

LITTLE SHOES

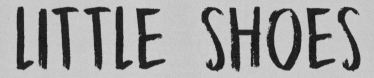

Find your oldest pair of shoes and draw around one of them in the space below. When you're a grown-up you'll be able to look back and feel amazed at how tiny your feet used to be.

HAPPY BIRTHDAY!

Can you remember your first birthday party? Keep a record of it here or use the prompts below to plan your ultimate birthday party.

DATE:

LOCATION:

FOOD:

GUESTS:

PARTY GAMES/ACTIVITIES:

DECORATIONS:

ANYTHING ELSE?

CHAPTER 2: MY FAMILY

There are lots of different types of families in the world and this chapter is all about yours. You might think of your family as the people you live with, the people you're related to, or the people you care most about.

FAMILY TREE

Fill these branches with pictures of the people in your family. Write their names in the spaces underneath the pictures and add a note about how they're connected to you, for example 'grandma', 'uncle' or 'brother'. Draw a picture of yourself in the space at the bottom of the page labelled 'me'.

ME

FAMILY FACT FILE

Choose three members of your family to interview and complete these family fact files. You might find out something about them that you didn't know before. Don't forget to draw a picture or stick a photo of them in the frames provided.

NAME:

FAVOURITE COLOUR:

FAVOURITE SONG:

HAPPIEST MEMORY:

BEST PIECE OF ADVICE:

FUNNIEST JOKE:

NAME:

FAVOURITE COLOUR:

FAVOURITE SONG:

HAPPIEST MEMORY:

BEST PIECE OF ADVICE:

FUNNIEST JOKE:

NAME:

FAVOURITE COLOUR:

FAVOURITE SONG:

HAPPIEST MEMORY:

BEST PIECE OF ADVICE:

FUNNIEST JOKE:

A DIFFERENT TIME

Ask the oldest person in your family if you can interview them about their childhood to find out what life was like in a different time. As well as writing down their answers, you could record the interview so that you'll be able to listen back to it in the future.

WHAT IS YOUR FULL NAME?

WHERE AND WHEN WERE YOU BORN?

WHO DID YOU LIVE WITH WHEN YOU WERE GROWING UP?

WHAT WAS IT LIKE AT YOUR SCHOOL?

WHAT KIND OF GAMES DID YOU PLAY?

WHAT WAS THE NAUGHTIEST THING YOU DID WHEN YOU WERE MY AGE?

DID YOU GO ON HOLIDAY? WHERE DID YOU GO?

WHAT NEW INVENTIONS HAVE THERE BEEN SINCE YOU WERE LITTLE?

WOULD YOU RATHER BE A CHILD NOW OR BACK WHEN YOU WERE GROWING UP?

FAMILY RITUALS

A ritual is a routine that has meaning. It's a tradition that your family has to celebrate or remember something. It might be connected to a religion, like putting up decorations around your house or eating special meals on festival days, or it could be something as simple as having pancakes for breakfast at the weekend. What rituals do your family have? Write or draw about them in the spaces below.

FAMILY POEM

An acrostic is a poem in which the first letter of each line spells out a word or phrase. Can you write an acrostic poem about your family? The lines can rhyme if you'd like them to, but they don't have to.

F

A

M

I

L

Y

PET PROFILE

Here's a place to write all about your pet. If you don't have a pet, make up some facts about a dream animal that you'd love to own.

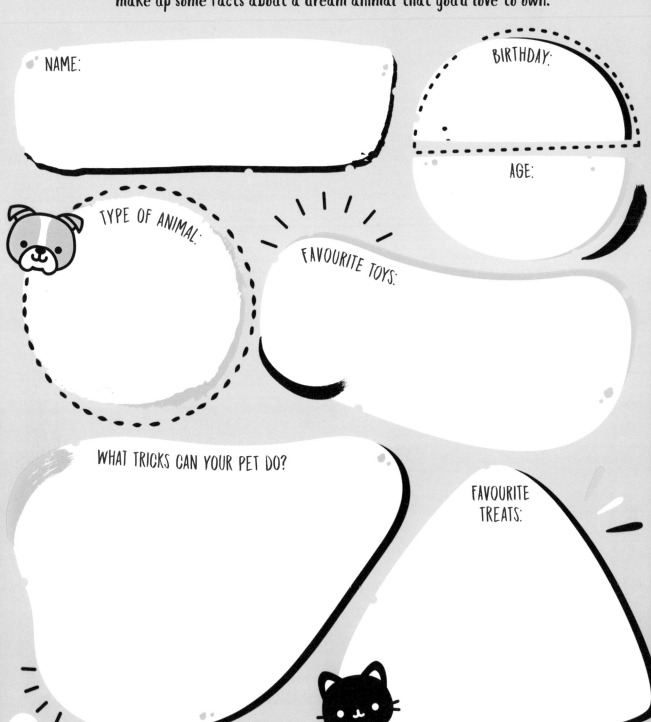

NAME:

BIRTHDAY:

AGE:

TYPE OF ANIMAL:

FAVOURITE TOYS:

WHAT TRICKS CAN YOUR PET DO?

FAVOURITE TREATS:

DOES YOUR PET HAVE ANY OTHER FURRY FRIENDS?

WHAT'S THE FUNNIEST THING YOUR PET DOES?

STICK IN A PHOTO OR DRAW A PICTURE OF YOUR PET BELOW:

PERFECT PET

If you could keep any type of animal as a pet, what would you choose? Fill in the top two rows below with your four favourite animals. Then, pick one animal from each pair and write your answers in the spaces provided. Keep choosing until you have just one left. This is your perfect pet!

PAIR 1

PAIR 2

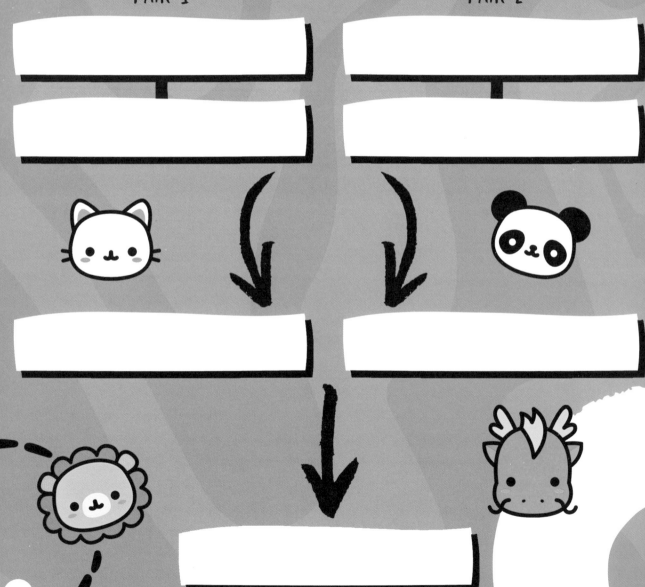

CHAPTER 3:
WHEN I WAS LITTLE

Can you remember what it was like being 3 or 4 years old? This chapter is all about the time when you were no longer a baby but weren't yet old enough to go to school.

Our memories of this special time often fade as we get older, so complete the activities on the following pages to keep a record and make sure you never forget!

KEEPING BUSY

What kind of things did you get up to when you were little? Tick the boxes and fill in the gaps.

Did anyone other than your parents help look after you? If yes, tick the box and write in their names.

☐ GRANDPARENTS

☐ FAMILY FRIENDS

☐ OLDER SIBLINGS

☐ CHILDMINDER / BABYSITTER / NANNY

☐ OTHER

Did you go to a preschool, nursery or kindergarten?

☐ YES, IT WAS CALLED:

☐ NO

Did you go to any classes, such as dance, music or football?

☐ YES, THE CLASSES I WENT TO WERE:

☐ NO

Which of the activities below did you do to keep busy at home?

- [ ] ARTS AND CRAFTS
- [ ] COOKING
- [ ] PLAYING WITH TOYS
- [ ] DOING PUZZLES
- [ ] DRESSING UP
- [ ] PLAYING COMPUTER GAMES
- [ ] READING BOOKS OR LISTENING TO STORIES

- [ ] DANCING
- [ ] LISTENING TO MUSIC
- [ ] WATCHING TV
- [ ] OTHER (WRITE WHAT IT WAS IN THE SPACE BELOW)

....

....

Where was your favourite place to go out? Perhaps you loved going to the play park, visiting friends, or having a snack in a café. Stick a photo or draw a picture of yourself in the place you loved best and add a caption to explain where you were and what you used to do there.

MINI-ME MEMORIES

Cast your mind back to the days before you were old enough to go to school. What can you remember? Write in these spaces to make a record of a time when you did each of the following things. Ask a family member for help remembering if you need to.

MADE A MESS:

DID SOMETHING FUNNY:

MADE A NEW FRIEND:

DID SOMETHING FOR THE FIRST TIME:

SAID SOMETHING SWEET:

HURT YOURSELF:

FELT REALLY HAPPY:

CELEBRATED A BIRTHDAY:

FIRST FRIENDS

Can you remember the children you used to play with at nursery school, or out and about when you were little? Fill the frames with photos or drawings of your first friends. Write the name of each friend in the space below, and colour in the balloon if you still know them now.

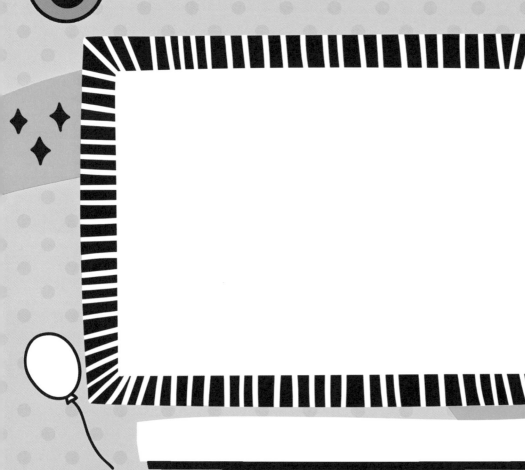

LITTLE LIKES

What did you like to play, watch, sing, read and do when you were little? Draw or write about the things you liked best in the spaces provided. Colour in the stars to show how much you still like those things now.

FAVOURITE GAME:

☆☆☆

FAVOURITE TOY:

☆☆☆

FAVOURITE BOOK:

☆☆☆

FAVOURITE MOVIE OR TV SHOW:

☆☆☆

FAVOURITE SONG:

☆☆☆

FAVOURITE COLOUR:

☆☆☆

FAVOURITE FOOD:

☆☆☆

FAVOURITE CLOTHES:

☆☆☆

FAVOURITE ANIMAL:

☆☆☆

THEN AND NOW

Learning new skills can be challenging and frustrating, but when you master the skill, it feels so good! Tick to record which of these you first learned when you were little, which you have learned since then, and which you are learning now.

SKILL	COULD DO WHEN I WAS LITTLE	CAN DO NOW	LEARNING HOW TO DO
TIE SHOELACES			
POUR JUICE FROM A CARTON			
RIDE A BICYCLE			
SWIM 5 METRES			
SPREAD BUTTER ON TOAST			
COUNT MONEY			
TELL THE TIME			
PUT ON A JUMPER			
FALL ASLEEP ON MY OWN			

CHAPTER 4:
HOME AND AWAY

There's no place like home and there's nothing like a holiday! This chapter is all about the place you live — where it is and what it's like.

There's also space to record details of anywhere you've been away from home and the places in the world you'd like to visit.

POST IT!

Where do you live? Can you fill in the envelope so that it would find its way to you if you put it in a postbox? Don't forget to include the number you live at, the name of the road you live on, the town or city that you live in, the country, and your postcode.

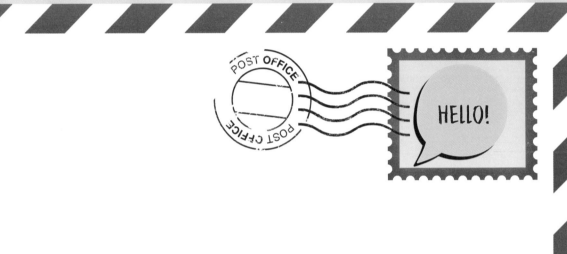

Use the boxes below to design your own unique stamps:

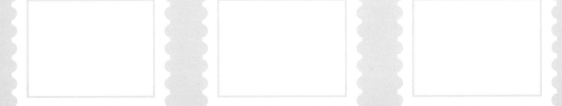

A PICTURE
OF HOME

Draw a picture or stick a photo of the
place you live in the space below.

MAP MASTER

Use this space to draw a map of where you live. Start by drawing your home, then see if you can work out where other landmarks near you should go. Where is your school? The nearest shop? Your local park? Can you draw on roads and write in the names of the streets?

HOME FACT FILE

Answer the questions below to make a record of the place where you live.

WHAT TYPE OF HOME DO YOU LIVE IN?
(Flat, house, bungalow, etc.)

WHAT COLOUR IS YOUR FRONT DOOR?

HOW MANY BEDROOMS DOES IT HAVE?

WHAT'S YOUR FAVOURITE ROOM?

WHERE'S THE BEST PLACE TO HIDE?

WHERE'S THE COMFIEST PLACE TO SIT?

DO YOU HAVE A GARDEN OR ANY OUTDOOR SPACE? WHAT'S IT LIKE?

BEDROOM PLAN

Imagine that you are looking down on your bedroom. Can you draw where everything is from above? Here's an example of what it might look like:

DREAM BEDROOM

Which of these cool things would you love to have in your dream bedroom? Colour them in, then draw smiley faces in the circles next to your favourites.

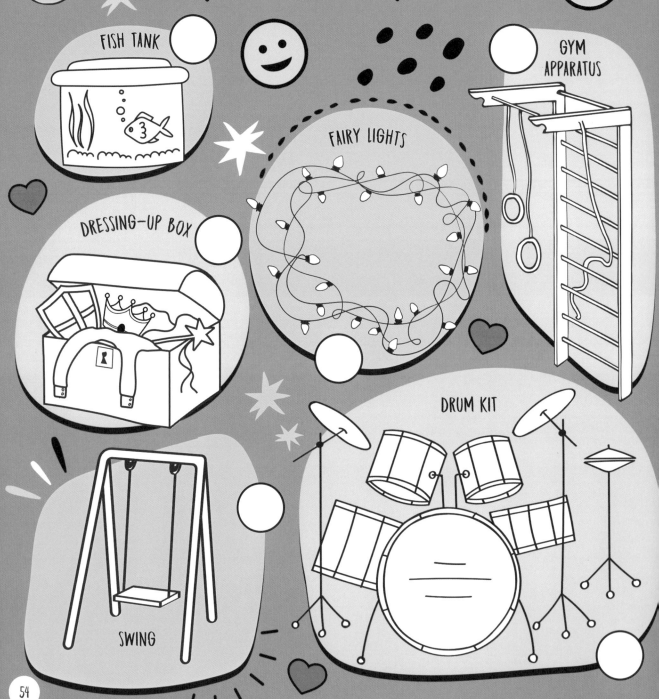

FISH TANK

GYM APPARATUS

FAIRY LIGHTS

DRESSING-UP BOX

DRUM KIT

SWING

54

WORLD MAP

HAMSTER

BED WITH SLIDE

BOOK CASE

TELESCOPE

HOLLYWOOD MIRROR

DOG

DESK

BEAN BAG

55

WOULD YOU RATHER — HOME

Read each of the choices below and make a decision. Would you rather ...

LIVE IN A TREEHOUSE? ☐	OR	LIVE ON A RIVERBOAT? ☐
LIVE IN A HOME THAT WAS REVOLTINGLY SMELLY? ☐	OR	LIVE IN A HOME THAT WAS REVOLTINGLY SLIMY? ☐
LIVE AT THE TOP OF A SKYSCRAPER? ☐	OR	LIVE AT THE TOP OF A MOUNTAIN? ☐
HAVE A SLIDE FROM YOUR BEDROOM TO THE STREET? ☐	OR	HAVE A TRAMPOLINE ON YOUR ROOF? ☐
LIVE IN A HAUNTED HOUSE? ☐	OR	LIVE IN AN OGRE'S SWAMP? ☐
LIVE IN A BOUNCY CASTLE? ☐	OR	LIVE IN A GIANT SANDCASTLE? ☐
HAVE A CINEMA IN YOUR HOME? ☐	OR	HAVE A SWIMMING POOL IN YOUR HOME? ☐
SHARE YOUR HOME WITH UNICORNS? ☐	OR	SHARE YOUR HOME WITH DINOSAURS? ☐

WOULD YOU RATHER — AWAY

Now try these. Would you rather ...

HAVE WINGS THAT WOULD LET YOU FLY OFF ON HOLIDAY? ☐	OR	HAVE POWERS TO MAGIC YOURSELF TO ANYWHERE IN THE WORLD? ☐
GO ON A BEACH TRIP? ☐	OR	GO ON AN ADVENTURE HOLIDAY? ☐
FORGET YOUR TOOTHBRUSH? ☐	OR	FORGET YOUR PANTS? ☐
VISIT THE MOON IN A SPACESHIP? ☐	OR	TRAVEL TO THE BOTTOM OF THE SEA IN A SUBMARINE? ☐
SAIL AROUND THE WORLD? ☐	OR	SWIM ACROSS THE ATLANTIC OCEAN? ☐
TRAVEL BY HELICOPTER? ☐	OR	TRAVEL BY JET SKI? ☐
GO ON A DAY OUT TO A THEME PARK? ☐	OR	GO ON A DAY OUT TO A WATER PARK? ☐
CLIMB THE TALLEST MOUNTAIN? ☐	OR	ABSEIL DOWN THE DEEPEST CANYON? ☐

HOLIDAY POSTCARDS

Draw or write on the postcards to show all the different places you've visited — either on holiday or on a day out. They could be places close to home or far away.

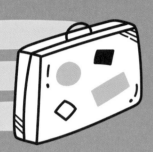

ULTIMATE DAY OUT

Which of these famous sites and places would you love to go to? Number them from 1 to 10, with the one you'd most like to visit at number 1.

WALT DISNEY WORLD®
At this entertainment resort in Florida, United States of America, you can see all of your favourite Disney® characters come to life.

THE EIFFEL TOWER
This tower in Paris, France, is one of the most famous structures in the world. It weighs over 10,000 tonnes — that's the same as 95 blue whales, the largest mammals on Earth.

SAN DIEGO ZOO
This zoo in sunny California, USA, is home to over 12,000 amazing animals.

STONEHENGE
This huge circle of standing stones in Salisbury, England, was built by humans over many hundreds of years. Some of the largest stones weigh a whopping 22 tonnes.

LEGOLAND®
LEGOLAND® California, in the USA, has over 30,000 LEGO®
models made from more than 62 million LEGO® bricks.

MOUNT EVEREST
Located in the Himalayas, a mountain range in Asia, this mountain is the highest in the
world. Every year, it attracts hundreds of daring adventurers from all over the globe.

THE GREAT PYRAMID OF GIZA
This pyramid in Egypt has stood for thousands of years and is made up of
over 2 million stones. It was built as a tomb for the ruler of ancient Egypt.

THE LEANING TOWER OF PISA
This bell tower in Pisa, Italy, is famous for the way it leans over to
one side, which is due to the way it was built many hundreds of years ago.

THE COLOSSEUM
The ancient Romans loved watching sport and so built themselves this arena.
Events included gladiator combats, chariot races and even pretend ship battles.

THE SCIENCE MUSEUM
This museum in London, England, is one of the city's biggest tourist attractions,
offering live science shows, interactive play areas and even an IMAX® cinema.

TRAVEL TALES

Answer the questions below to create a record of the last holiday you went on, your favourite place and where you'd like to go next!

WHERE WAS THE LAST PLACE YOU WENT ON HOLIDAY OR FOR A DAY OUT?

WOULD YOU GO THERE AGAIN?

YES ☐   NO ☐

WHY?

WHERE IS YOUR FAVOURITE PLACE YOU'VE EVER BEEN?

WHAT DID YOU LIKE ABOUT IT?

IF YOU COULD GO ANYWHERE IN THE WORLD RIGHT NOW, WHERE WOULD YOU GO?

WHAT WOULD YOU PACK?

WHO WOULD YOU TAKE WITH YOU?

CHAPTER 5: ALL ABOUT ME

This chapter is all about someone amazing — you!
You are unique and you are changing all the time
— growing up and learning new things — so in this
chapter there is space for you to record exactly
what you're like right here, right now. Have fun!

SELF PORTRAIT

Using a mirror or a photograph, draw a picture of your face in the frame below. Try to draw exactly what you see, not what you think is there!

EYE CLOSE-UP

The coloured part of your eye is called the iris and you may have
noticed that it's not just one colour. Grab a mirror and take a look
at your eyes, then copy what you see on to the drawing below.
Think carefully about all the different shades you can see.

Now ask a friend or family member if you can look
at their eyes and copy what you see below:

THESE EYES BELONG TO:

FOOT FACT FILE

How often do you stop to think about your feet? They work so hard carrying you around all day and deserve some respect! Use these pages to record all the details of your fantastic feet. Draw around your foot in the space below.

GET A RULER AND MEASURE YOUR DRAWING. HOW LONG IS YOUR FOOT?

HOW SMELLY ARE YOUR FEET? RATE THEM ON THIS SMELLOMETER!

SERIOUSLY STINKY

5 — ☐
4 — ☐
3 — ☐
2 — ☐
1 — ☐
0 — ☐

NOT SMELLY AT ALL

WHAT SHOE SIZE ARE YOU?

WHAT ARE YOUR FAVOURITE KINDS OF SHOES TO WEAR? RATE THESE FROM 1 TO 5 WITH YOUR FAVOURITE AT NUMBER 1:

SANDALS ☐
SLIPPERS ☐
WELLINGTON BOOTS ☐
TRAINERS ☐
SCHOOL SHOES ☐

WHAT DID THE LAST PAIR OF SHOES YOU PUT ON LOOK LIKE? DRAW A PICTURE OF THEM HERE:

FINGER FUN

You see your hands every day, but how well do you actually know them? Spend some time really looking at your hands and get to know your fabulous fingers with these fun activities!

Stretch out your hand and draw around it in the space below. Draw on your fingernails and any distinguishing features like moles or scars.

When your hand is stretched out like this, the distance from the tip of your little finger to the tip of your thumb is called your span. Get a ruler and measure this distance, then record the length of your span here:

Now measure from the bottom of your wrist to the tip of your middle finger, and record the height of your hand here:

Everyone in the world has a unique fingerprint. Record yours here by colouring in the pad of one of your fingers with a felt tip pen. Then, while the ink is still wet, press your fingertip onto the page.

Do you know any tricks, rhymes or songs where you use your fingers? If so, write them down here:

IF NOT, HERE'S ONE YOU CAN TRY:

Fool your friends into thinking you have eleven fingers with this easy trick! Pointing with the index finger of your right hand, touch each finger of your left hand, counting out loud 'one, two, three, four, five.' Now point with the index finger of your left hand, and touch each finger of your right hand, this time counting down 'ten, nine, eight, seven, six.' 5 plus 6 equals 11!

CAN YOU, OR CAN'T YOU?

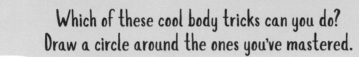

Which of these cool body tricks can you do?
Draw a circle around the ones you've mastered.

ROLL YOUR TONGUE

WHISTLE

CROSS YOUR EYES

RAISE ONE EYEBROW

WIGGLE YOUR EARS

CLICK YOUR FINGERS

TOUCH THE TIP OF YOUR NOSE WITH THE TIP OF YOUR TONGUE

SUPERPOWER SHOWDOWN

Would you like to be able to fly, turn invisible or have X-ray vision? Think of four superpowers you'd love to have and write them in the first two rows below, then choose the one from each pair that you would most like to have. Out of the final two, choose which superpower wins the showdown!

PAIR 1

PAIR 2

I AM ...

How would you describe yourself? Colour around
the words that match your personality.

CALM

UNIQUE

TIDY

QUIET

CONSIDERATE

ENERGETIC

LOUD

ADVENTUROUS

FRIENDLY

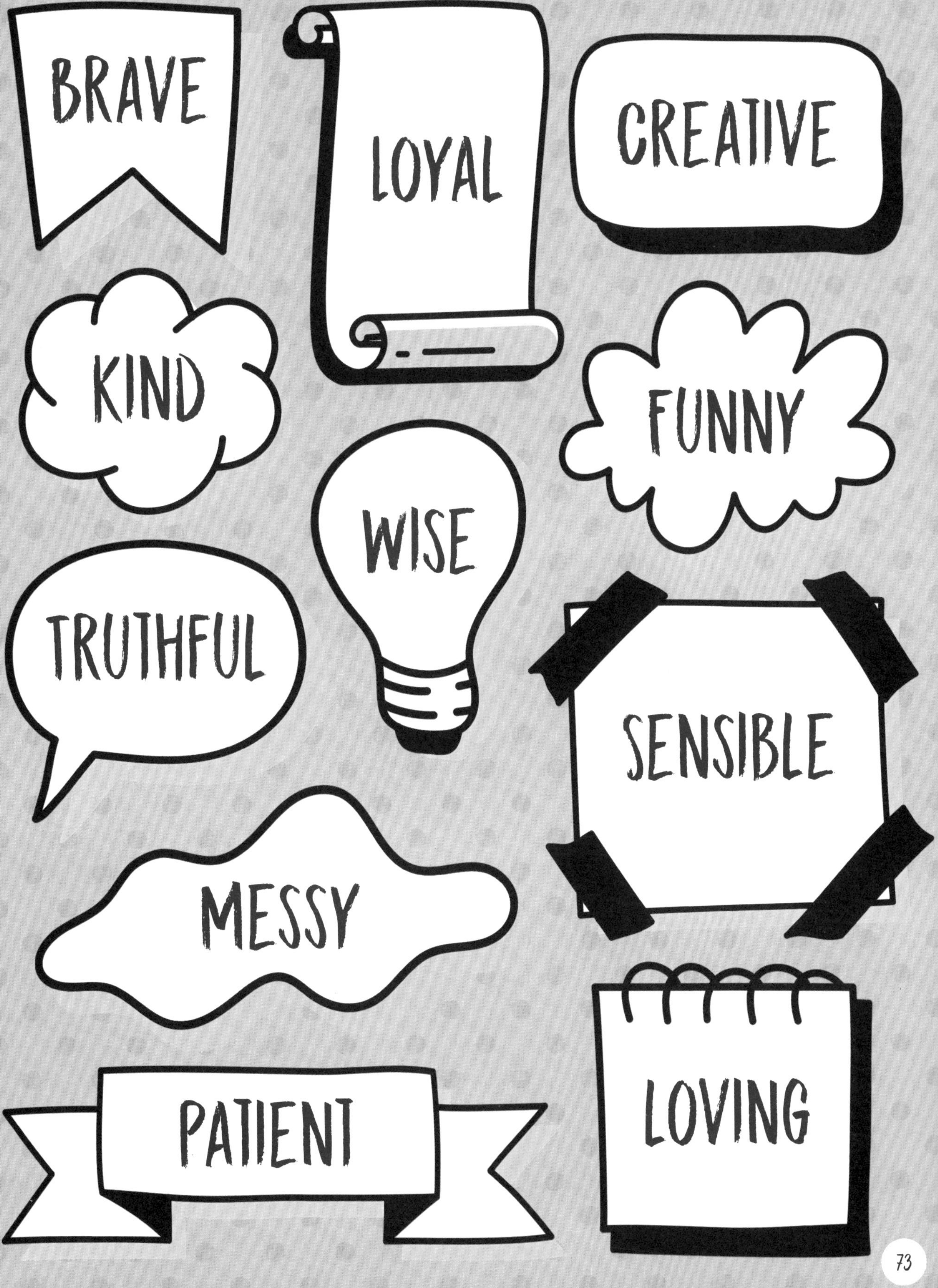

BRAVE

LOYAL

CREATIVE

KIND

FUNNY

WISE

TRUTHFUL

SENSIBLE

MESSY

PATIENT

LOVING

HOW THEY SEE ME

How do your friends and loved ones see you? Ask them to write a few words that describe you in the glasses below. Don't forget to ask them to include their name so you know who wrote what.

WRITTEN BY:

WRITTEN BY:

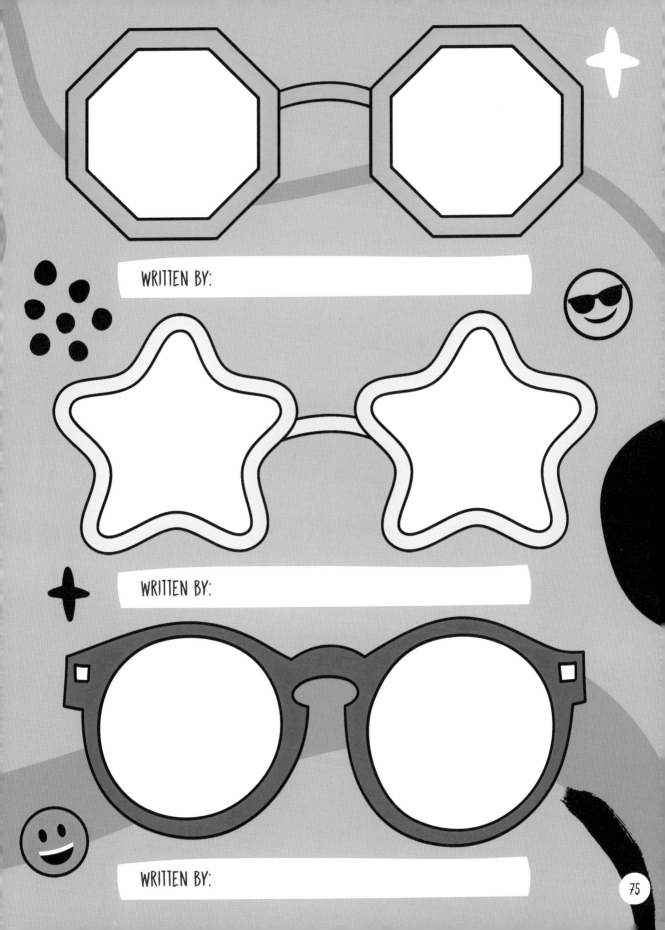

WRITTEN BY:

WRITTEN BY:

WRITTEN BY:

A LETTER TO YOUR FUTURE SELF

Imagine yourself in exactly one years' time. Complete this letter below so that your future self can look back and remember what it felt like to be you right here, right now.

Dear future me,

I am writing this letter from the year .... , and I am .... years old.

Right now, I can see .... ,

hear .... and smell

....

I feel .... My three favourite

things right now are .... ,

.... and

.... The last person I hugged

was .... and the last person

I spoke to on the phone was ....

Tomorrow I am going to ....

Here is a joke that makes me laugh: ....

....

FUTURE ME: Do you still find it funny?   YES ☐   NO ☐

Love from, ...

CHAPTER 6: MY SCHOOL

There are lots of different types of school — enormous schools with thousands of children, tiny schools where children of different ages are all in one class, boarding schools where the children stay overnight, home schools where children are taught by their parents and many more! This chapter is all about your school — what it's like, and how you feel about it.

SCHOOL FACT FILE

Use this page to make a record of all the important details about your school.

SCHOOL NAME:

SCHOOL LOGO —
DRAW IT HERE:

NAME OF YOUR TEACHER:

HOW YOU GET TO SCHOOL:

DO YOU TAKE A PACKED LUNCH
OR HAVE SCHOOL DINNERS?:

NUMBER OF
CHILDREN IN
YOUR CLASS:

BEST THING ABOUT YOUR SCHOOL:

WHAT DO YOU WEAR TO SCHOOL?
DRAW YOURSELF WEARING IT HERE:

WORST THING ABOUT YOUR SCHOOL:

NUMBER OF CHILDREN IN YOUR WHOLE SCHOOL:

FAVOURITE LESSONS

Are there some lessons you absolutely love and others that you can't wait to be over? Order these lessons from 1 to 10, with your favourite lesson at number 1 and your least favourite at number 10.

ART AND DESIGN	ENGLISH	HISTORY	MATHS	MUSIC
COMPUTING	GEOGRAPHY	LANGUAGES	SCIENCE	PHYSICAL EDUCATION

1.

2.

3.

4.

5.

6.

7.

8.

9.

10.

IF YOU HAVE A FAVOURITE LESSON THAT'S NOT LISTED ABOVE, WRITE THE NAME OF IT HERE:

WHAT IS IT THAT YOU LIKE ABOUT YOUR FAVOURITE LESSON?

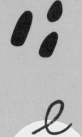

SCHOOL FRIENDS GALLERY

Ask your school friends to draw pictures of themselves in these frames and to sign their masterpieces on the lines below.

CLASS AWARDS

Think carefully about the people in your class and decide who you think should win each of the trophies below. You can give more than one award to the same person, and you should give yourself some, too! Write the name of the award winners in the space under each trophy.

HELPING OTHERS

NEVER GIVING UP

BEING CURIOUS

HAVING GOOD IDEAS

MAKING UP GAMES

BEING FUNNY

BEING CREATIVE

SHARING

BEING FRIENDLY

SOLVING PROBLEMS

83

TYPICAL TIMETABLE

Does your school day normally have a routine that you follow? For example, do you usually start and finish at the same time, and have breaks and eat lunch at the same time most days? Use this timetable to create a record of what a typical day at your school is like, adding in what you do at different times.

TIME:	WHAT HAPPENS
	Arrive at school

P.E. POWER

What sports or physical activities do you like to do at school?
Write down four that you love in the first two rows below,
then choose the one from each pair that you enjoy the most.
Next, choose which of the final two is your favourite and
write your ultimate P.E. power in the space at the bottom.

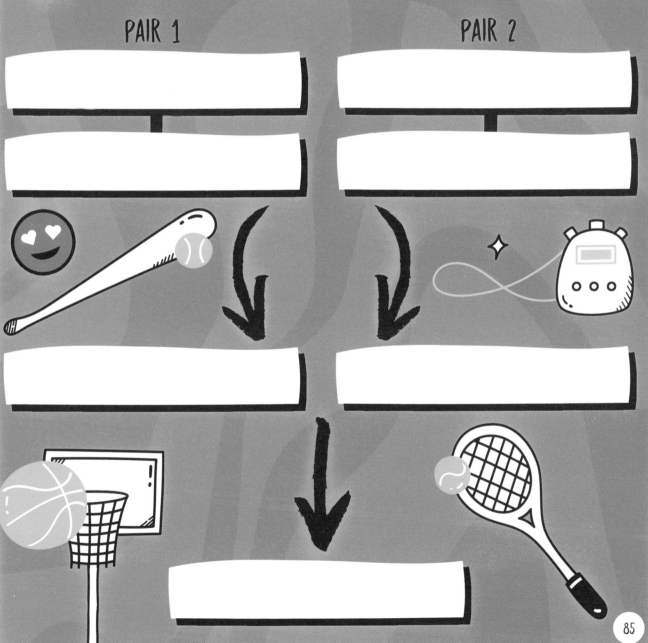

PAIR 1   PAIR 2

FAVOURITE TEACHERS

Draw pictures of your favourite teachers in the frames below. Then, write a few words about what they were like or a memory from the time you spent with them. Save the biggest frame for the best teacher you've ever had and write down why they're your absolute favourite.

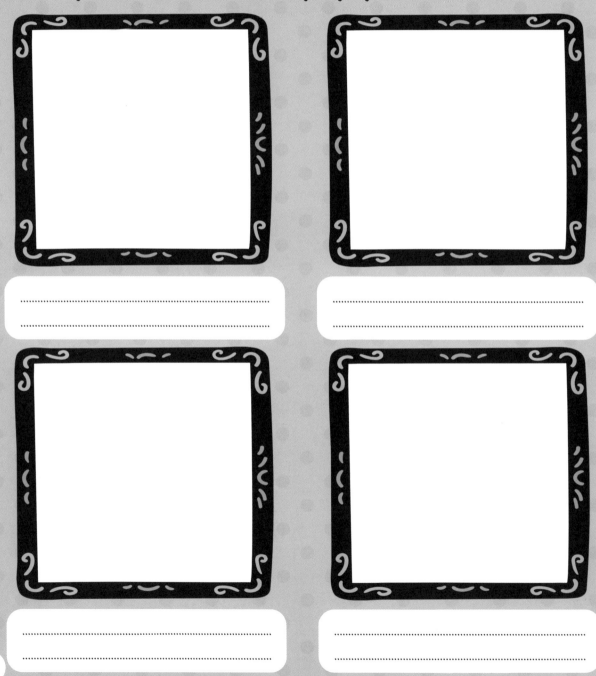

PLAYGROUND MAP

Draw a map of your school playground here. Perhaps there's an area for playing football, or eating outside, or an area where only the older kids are allowed to go. Draw a star to show the place where you most like to play.

PLAYTIME DIARY

Write down the games you play at break, lunchtime or after school every day for a week. At the end of the week, draw a circle around the day you enjoyed the most!

MONDAY

TUESDAY

WEDNESDAY

THURSDAY

FRIDAY

CHAPTER 7: A DAY IN MY LIFE

This chapter is all about the things going on in your life at the moment — the way you spend your days and fill your time. You might have some big, exciting things going on and there's space to record those, but the small things are just as important. Record all the little details here!

GOOD MORNING

What is your routine when you get up in the morning? Number these activities from 1 to 10 to show the order you usually do things in. Add any activities of your own in the spaces provided. If there's anything here that you don't do, just cross it out.

Activity	
BRUSH TEETH	
WASH	
SAY GOOD MORNING TO THE PEOPLE YOU LIVE WITH	
HAVE BREAKFAST	
GET DRESSED	
BRUSH HAIR	
GO TO THE TOILET	
PACK SCHOOLBAG	

The time I usually get up is: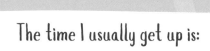

....

My favourite food to have for breakfast is:

....

My favourite thing to do in the morning is:

....

SUNRISE COLOURING

Colour this calming pattern to get you in the mood for an awesome day ahead.

MY FAVOURITE DAY

Think of a day you've had recently that you really loved and that left you with a big smile on your face! It could be anything from a relaxing day chilling out at home to one spent trying a new sport or visiting friends. Record your memories of the day in the spaces below and return to it whenever you need cheering up.

WHERE YOU WERE THAT DAY:

WHAT YOU DID THERE:

THE PEOPLE YOU SPENT TIME WITH:

WHAT THE WEATHER WAS LIKE:

THE THINGS YOU ATE AND DRANK:

ANYTHING SPECIAL THAT HAPPENED:

YOUR FAVOURITE MEMORY FROM THE DAY:

HOW THE DAY MADE YOU FEEL:

WONDERFUL WEEKENDS

What kinds of things do you like to get up to at the weekend? Next weekend, make a record of everything you do in the spaces below. You could include the games you play, places you go, people you see and things you eat -- all the fun things that make up your time.

SATURDAY MORNING	SATURDAY AFTERNOON	SATURDAY EVENING

SUNDAY MORNING	SUNDAY AFTERNOON	SUNDAY EVENING

MAKE PLANS FOR NEXT WEEKEND:

PLANS FOR THE YEAR

Use this space to make a record of your plans for the months ahead. Perhaps there's a celebration you're looking forward to, like a friend's birthday, or a trip that you're excited to go on. Write down the months in the boxes provided to create your very own calendar.

MONTH: ....

MONTH: ....

MONTH: ....

MONTH: ....

MONTH: ....

MONTH: ....

MONTH: ....

MONTH: ....

MONTH: ....

MONTH: ....

MONTH: ....

MONTH: ....

7 DAYS OF DINNER

Draw and write what you have for your evening meal every day this week on the plates and in the spaces below. At the end of the week, put a star by the meal that was your favourite.

MONDAY:

TUESDAY:

WEDNESDAY:

THURSDAY:

FRIDAY:

SATURDAY:

SUNDAY:

READ ALL ABOUT IT!

Is there anything going on in your life at the moment that you'd like to tell the world? Fill in this front page to share your news.

HEADLINE: Can you think of a catchy title for your story? Headlines sometimes include alliteration (where each word starts with the same letter) — such as 'Sister Steals Sandwich in Shocking Snack Scandal!'

MAIN STORY: Reel in your readers with a dramatic opening, for example 'Family members were shocked and appalled when a cheeky sister stole her brother's cheese sandwich.'

DESCRIBE WHAT HAPPENED: 'The sandwich was left unguarded when the brother went to fetch a drink, and this is when the terrible theft took place.' You could also include a quote from someone involved. Finish by telling the reader how the story ended or what's going to happen next: 'Both the sister and the dad have been approached for comment. The brother is currently plotting a way to get his own back.' Draw a picture to go with your story.

SPORTS NEWS: Have you scored any goals or beaten your personal best recently? Or are you going to be taking part in any sports activities over the next few weeks? Tell the reader about them here. Draw a picture to go with your story.

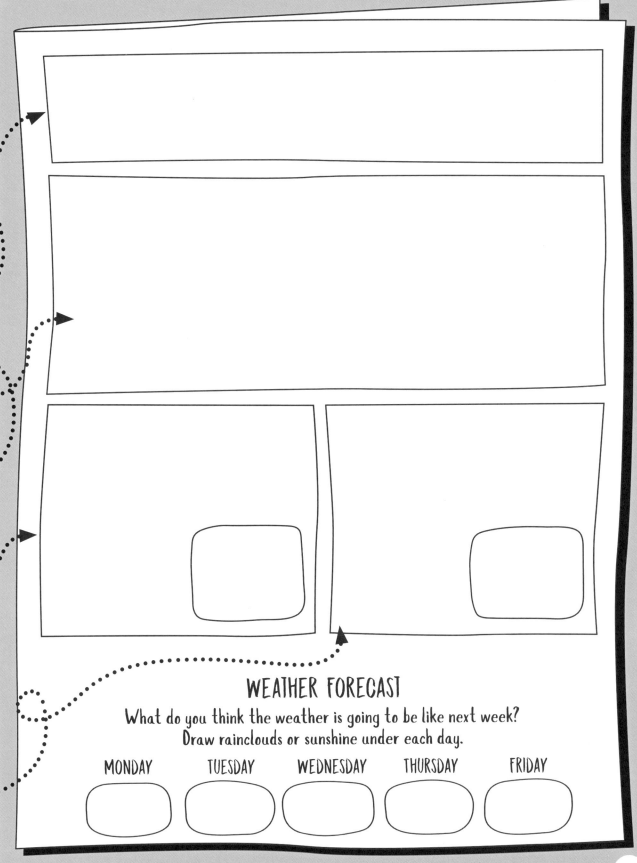

WEATHER FORECAST

What do you think the weather is going to be like next week?
Draw rainclouds or sunshine under each day.

MONDAY	TUESDAY	WEDNESDAY	THURSDAY	FRIDAY

SLEEP STORIES

A good night's sleep is so important for your body and mind. How do you wind down at the end of the day? Colour in the pillows to show which of these dreamy techniques you use to let your body know it's time for sleep.

TAKE A WARM BATH

LISTEN TO CALMING MUSIC

FLUFF UP YOUR PILLOWS

DIM THE LIGHTS

CUDDLE UP WITH A TOY OR BLANKET

READ A BOOK

CHANGE INTO PYJAMAS

AVOID SCREENS

What time do you normally start getting ready for bed?

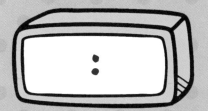

What time do you usually fall asleep?

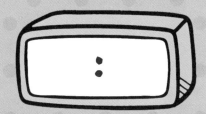

Write the names of your favourite bedtime stories on the front of these books:

Colour in the positions below that you like to sleep in:

DREAM DIARY

Can you remember any of your dreams? Write or draw about them in the clouds below. If you can't remember any right now, you could try keeping this book and a pen by your bed and recording your dreams as soon as you wake up.

CHAPTER 8: MY FAVOURITES

Everyone has unique tastes — they're part of what make you, you. Use this chapter to create a record of all the things you love most in the world, from music and movies, to books, food and hobbies. There's even space to record your favourite things about yourself.

TOP 5

What are your top five favourite songs? Create your own music chart by ordering them from one to five, with your favourite at number one. Include both the name of the song and the singer or band.

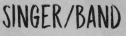

SINGER/BAND	SONG
1.	
2.	
3.	
4.	
5.	

LYRICS

Write out the words from your favourite song
below and decorate them with your own drawings.

BOOK REVIEWS

Use the pages of these books to write down what you think about the next three stories you read. Whether you love them or hate them, write down your honest opinion and give each one a rating out of three stars.

HINT:
Did the characters feel real?

HINT:
Did the story grip you and make you want to keep turning the pages?

☆☆☆

TITLE:

AUTHOR:

TITLE: _____ AUTHOR: _____

TITLE: _____ AUTHOR: _____

MOVIE MAGIC

Draw a poster advertising your favourite movie in the space below.

What is your favourite snack to
eat while watching a movie?

....

Where is your favourite place to watch
a movie? Maybe it's at the cinema, or
chilling on your sofa, or even in bed!

....

TOP TV

Write the names of your favourite TV shows
or YouTube channels on the screens below.

FREE TIME FAVOURITES

What hobbies do you like to take part in when you have free time? Colour in each of the pictures using this code:

- I love to do this!
- I quite like doing this
- I don't like doing this
- I've never done this but I'd love to give it a go!
- I've never done this and I don't want to try it!

SWIMMING

TRAMPOLINING

PLAYING FOOTBALL

CYCLING

GYMNASTICS

SINGING

DANCING

ACTING

ART

ROLLERSKATING

GAMING

CODING

PLAYING A MUSICAL INSTRUMENT

BAKING

READING

Write a bit more about your favourite hobbies and the things you like to do in your free time here:

FAVOURITE FOODS

What would you have in your ultimate meal?
Fill the plates with drawings of what
you'd choose for each course.

DRINK:

STARTER:

MAIN COURSE:

SIDE DISH:

DESSERT:

Now imagine that you had to choose just one ultimate favourite food. What would it be? Write down four of your favourite foods in the spaces on the first row, then choose which from each pair you like the best and write it in the second row. Out of the final two, decide which you think is the tastiest food in the whole world!

PAIR 1 PAIR 2

My ultimate favourite food is:			

THINGS I LIKE MOST ABOUT ME

We are all unique and special, and we all have good qualities and things that we're particularly talented at doing. What are the things that you like most about yourself? Perhaps you're brilliant at magic tricks or you're a really loyal friend. Write the top five things you like about yourself in the spaces below.

1.

2.

3.

4.

5.

CHAPTER 9: THE FUTURE

What do you think the future will be like? What kind of person do you want to become? What are your goals for the weeks, months and years ahead, and what could you do now to work towards achieving them? This chapter will help you think about all these important questions.

WISHES FOR THE FUTURE

What are your hopes and dreams for the future? You might have big dreams for the whole world, hopes for your family and friends, and goals for your own life. Fill the clouds with your wishes for the future and maybe they'll come true!

STEPS TO SUCCESS

Think of some goals you'd like to achieve in the next few weeks or months and write them in the spaces below. Perhaps you'd like to make a new friend or learn how to count to ten in another language. Next, think about which step you're on at the moment for each goal. Do you think you can do it? Each time you go up a step towards achieving your goal, colour it in.

GOAL:

I DID IT!

I'M GOING TO DO IT

I KNOW I CAN DO IT

I'LL TRY TO DO IT

I'M WORKING OUT HOW I DO IT

I WANT TO DO IT

GOAL:

I DID IT!

I'M GOING TO DO IT

I KNOW I CAN DO IT

I'LL TRY TO DO IT

I'M WORKING OUT HOW I DO IT

I WANT TO DO IT

GOAL:

I DID IT!

I'M GOING TO DO IT

I KNOW I CAN DO IT

I'LL TRY TO DO IT

I'M WORKING OUT HOW I DO IT

I WANT TO DO IT

DEAR FUTURE ME ...

Imagine yourself as a grown-up. What kind of life do you want to be living? Will the things that are important to you now still be important to you then? Complete this letter to your future self so that you can look back at it and remember the person you hoped you'd become.

Dear future me,

I am writing this letter from the year .... and I am .... years old.

My greatest wish for the future is ....

....

When I am older, I want to live in ....

with ....

The job that I would like to do is ....

Sometimes grown-ups forget how to play and other important things they knew when they were young. I hope that you have never stopped

....

The best piece of advice I can give you is

....

Love from,

....

MAKE A TIME CAPSULE

A time capsule is a collection of objects that tell the story of what life is like now. Follow these simple instructions to make your own, then bury it in your garden or keep it hidden for the next few years. Your future self will love opening it!

1. FIND A CONTAINER.
If you're planning to bury your time capsule, make sure you get permission. It needs to be in something strong and watertight. If you'd prefer to keep it hidden away indoors then a cardboard box would work well. This way, you'll be able to take it with you if you ever move house.

2. DECORATE YOUR TIME CAPSULE.
You could write an instruction on it, like 'DO NOT OPEN UNTIL THE YEAR 2035'.

3. COLLECT OBJECTS TO PUT IN YOUR TIME CAPSULE.
Make sure you don't include anything that could go mouldy, that belongs to someone else or that you might need in future! Here are some ideas for what you could include:

- Something with today's date
- A small toy
- Newspaper clippings
- A recent photograph of you with your friends or family
- A drawing, painting or poem by you
- Coins from the current year
- A letter to your future self

4. BURY THE TIME CAPSULE OR HIDE IT AWAY FOR AS LONG AS YOU LIKE.

THE FUTURE STARTS NOW

Want to set yourself up for a positive future? Choose a few of these powerful phrases to repeat to yourself whenever you need a boost. If there are any that stand out to you, why not turn them into a poster for your bedroom?

I CAN DO THIS!

I BELIEVE IN MYSELF

MISTAKES HELP ME LEARN

TODAY IS A GOOD DAY TO TRY SOMETHING NEW

I CAN COPE WHEN THINGS GO WRONG

I AM LOVED

EVERYTHING IS DIFFICULT BEFORE IT IS EASY

ANYTHING I DON'T KNOW IS SOMETHING I CAN LEARN

NEVER GIVE UP!

IT'S COOL TO BE KIND

I AM CAPABLE OF AMAZING THINGS

THE MORE I PRACTISE THE BETTER I'LL GET